JOY AN IRISH CHRISTMAS

KEITH & KRISTYN GETTY

1. God Rest Ye Merry Gentlemen (with The Star of Munster)
2. Hark! the Herald Angels Sing (with Greengrass Reel)
3. What Child Is This?
4. Magnificat
5. How Suddenly a Baby Cries (with Narnian Reel)
6. Joy Has Dawned / Angels We Have Heard on High
7. Jesus, Joy of the Highest Heaven (A Children's Carol)
8. Carol of the Bells (with Young Tom Ennis Reel)
9. O Savior of Our Fallen Race
10. Fullness of Grace
11. Joy to the World (with Miss Eliza's Reel)
12. An Irish Christmas Blessing

GETTYMUSIC.COM

God Rest Ye Merry, Gentlemen

Traditional English Carol
Arranged by Keith Getty
& Fionán de Barra

Energetic Groove (♩=115)
Dm Gm/D Am/D
1. God rest you mer - ry, gen - tle - men, let noth - ing you dis - may; Re -
2. In Beth - le - hem, in Is - ra - el, this bless - ed Babe was born, and
3. From God our Heav - 'nly Fath - er a bless - ed an - gel came and
4. The shep - herds at those ti - dings re - joic - ed much in mind, and
5. Now to the Lord sing prais - es all you with - in this place, and
Dm Gm/D Am/D
mem - ber Christ, our Sa - vior, was born on Christ - mas Day to
laid with - in a man - ger up - on this bless - ed morn, the
un - to cer - tain shep - herds brought tid - ings of the same, how
left their flocks a - feed - ing in tem - pest, storm and wind and
with true love and broth - er - hood each oth - er now em - brace; This
Gm Am B♭maj7 C Refrain: Gm7 Am7
save us all from Sa - tan's pow'r when we were gone a - stray:
which His moth - er Ma - ry did noth - ing take in scorn:
that in Beth - le - hem was born the Son of God by name:
went to Beth - le - hem straight - way, the Son of God to find:
ho - ly tide of Christ - mas all oth - ers doth de - face:
O ti - dings of com - fort and
Dm Gm7 Am7 Dm C/D Dm C/D last time D5
joy, com - fort and joy, O ti - dings of com - fort and joy!
2. In
3. From
4. The
5. Now

STORIES BEHIND THE SONGS

God Rest Ye Merry Gentlemen (with The Star of Munster)

This carol dates back to the sixteenth century. It was considered so timeless that those who heard it throughout the years assumed it was a new song until the 1800s! At a time when church music was not always sung in the English language, this exemplifies how a carol told the Gospel story in words people understood. The song was famously used in Charles Dickens' "A Christmas Carol" and has been sung throughout the centuries to exuberantly wish Scrooge and countless others "tidings of comfort and joy." In our arrangement, we combined the carol with the Irish reel "The Star of Munster."

Hark! the Herald Angels Sing (with Greengrass Reel)

We wanted to arrange the carols in this collection to sound so joyful and energetic that listeners can't help but join the singing. This is the enthusiastic manner in which carols have been most commonly shared throughout history. Our version of "Hark! the Herald Angels Sing" includes an Irish-bluegrass influence. Many of our Nashville friends claim some of the best Irish musicians left Europe 200 years ago for America to live in the American South! We call the reel in this song "Greengrass" in honor of our friends Jeff, Buddy, Ron, Ross and Matt. Here's to the memorable evenings we spent at our home in Nashville playing music together.

What Child Is This?

This is a traditional English folk melody from the 16th century that was shared among the Celtic Islands and then fused with these lyrics in the 1800s. One of the little known facts about Celtic music is that it includes Spanish influences (particularly from the northern area of Galicia), so in this interpretation we approached the song with a melody from the traditional Basque carol "The Angel Gabriel."

Magnificat

The inspiration for this song comes from the Magnificat (the song of Mary in Luke 1). We wrote the melody during a stay in a log cabin in the Redwoods near San Francisco and then later crafted the lyrics with Stuart Townend. It was particularly poignant for Kristyn to sing the song while we were expecting our first daughter, Eliza Joy! Remarkably, Mary reaches beyond the miraculous personal news she receives to speak of the far-reaching wonder of God's faithfulness. We open this song with the "Wexford Carol" melody which is perhaps the best known Irish carol, performed here by Michael McGlynn and choral ensemble Anúna.

How Suddenly a Baby Cries (with Narnian Reel)

Dedicated to the memory of our friend, Derek Bingham (1946-2010)

This is a carol Kristyn wrote about how the coming of Christ affected the lives of individuals in the Gospel narrative, as well as how it continues to have an impact on lives throughout history. The melody comes from a traditional Irish folk tune called "The Star of the County Down" (County Down is a breathtaking area of Northern Ireland). The Irish writer C.S. Lewis once described his idea of heaven as "Oxford placed in the County Down." The grand imagery of Ireland later influenced his creation of Narnia-- a place which was "always winter and never Christmas" until the Lion roared. The reel Keith and Fionán wrote to accompany "How Suddenly" is aptly named "Narnian Reel."

Joy Has Dawned / Angels We Have Heard on High

Keith and Stuart Townend originally wrote "Joy Has Dawned" for a collection of hymns on the Apostle's Creed. Like many carols, Stuart's lyrics explain the Gospel story as the song develops. When we use this song in church services we combine it with one of our favorite carols, "Angels We Have Heard on High."

Hark! the Herald Angels Sing

Wesley, Whitfield & Mendelssohn
Arranged by Keith Getty,
Dave Cleaveland and Fionan de Barra

With Energy (♩ = 112)
F Dm B♭ Csus C Am B♭ F/C C F
1. Hark! the her - ald an - gels sing 'Glo - ry to the new - born King!
2. Christ, by high - est heav'n a - dored, Christ, the ev - er - last - ing Lord,
3. Hail the heav'n born Prince of Peace! Hail the Sun of right - eous - ness!
F Dm B♭ Csus C Am C Csus C G C
Peace on earth, and mer - cy mild, God and sin - ners re - con - ciled!'
late in time be - hold Him come, off - spring of a vir - gin's womb.
Light and life to all He brings, ris'n with heal - ing in His wings.
Am Dm Gm F/C C Am Dm Gm F/C C
Joy - ful, all ye na - tions rise, join the tri - umph of the skies,
Veiled in flesh the God - head see! Hail the in - car - nate De - i - ty!
Mild, He lays His glo - ry by; Born that man no more may die;
B♭ F/A Gm D7 Gm C F/A B♭ C D5
with the an - gel - ic host pro - claim, 'Christ is born in Beth - le - hem.'
Pleased as man with man to dwell, Je - sus, our Em-man - u - el.
Born to raise the sons of earth; Born to give them se - cond birth.

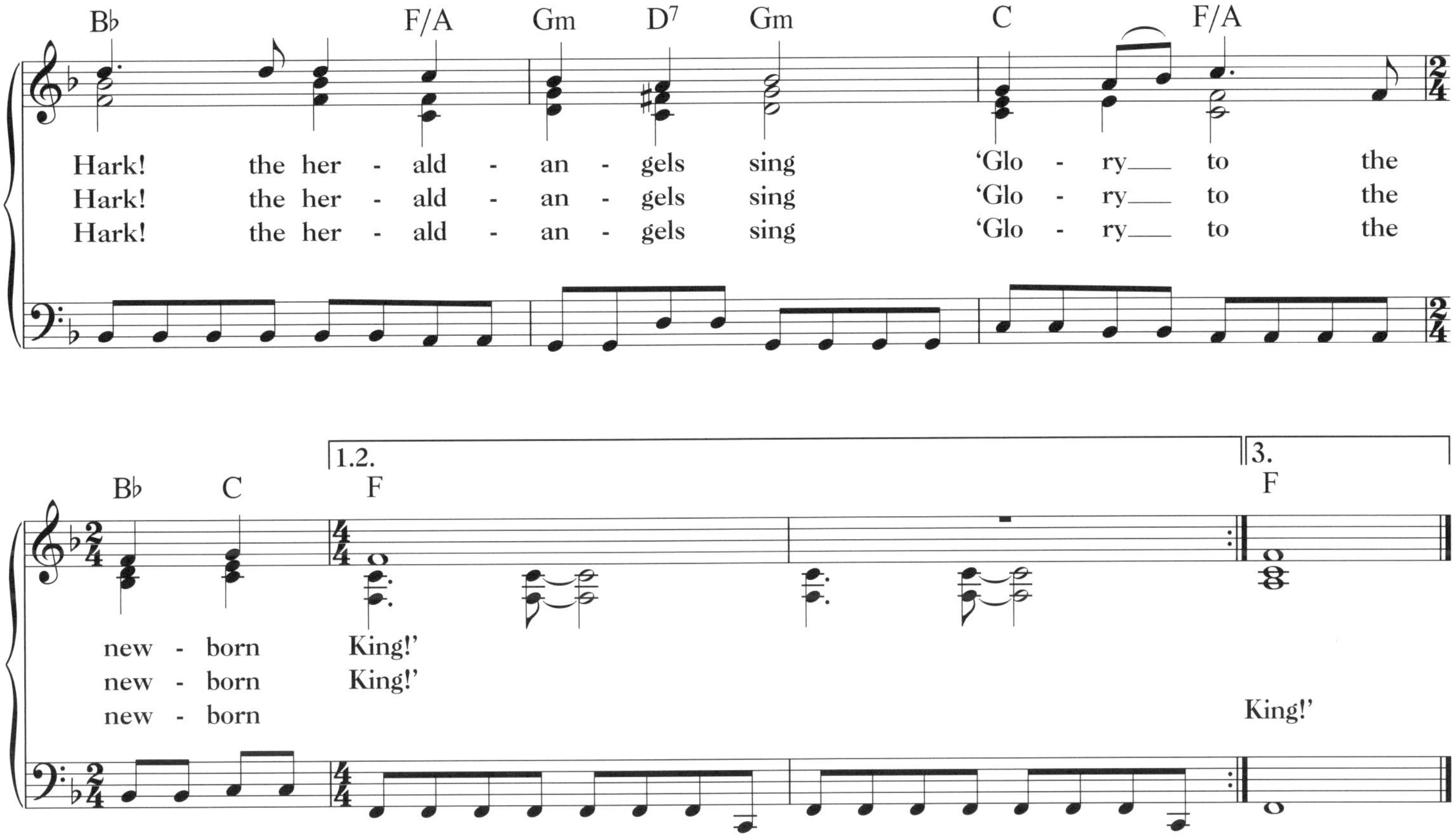
B♭ F/A Gm D7 Gm C F/A
Hark! the her - ald - an - gels sing 'Glo - ry to the
Hark! the her - ald - an - gels sing 'Glo - ry to the
Hark! the her - ald - an - gels sing 'Glo - ry to the
B♭ C 1.2. F 3. F
new - born King!'
new - born King!'
new - born King!'

What Child is This?

William Chatterton's Traditional English Carol
Arranged by Keith Getty and Fionán de Barra

Driving Rock Groove (♩ = 100)
Dm C/D B♭maj7/D A/D
1. What child is this who, laid to rest, On Ma - ry's lap is sleep - ing, Whom
2. Why lies he in such mean es - tate Where ox and ass are feed - ing? Good
3. So bring Him in - cense, gold and myrrh, come peas - ant, king to own Him; The
Dm C/D B♭ A Dm
an - gels greet with an - thems sweet While shep - herds watch are keep - ing?
Chris - tians fear: for sin - ners here The si - lent Word is plead - ing.
King of kings sal - va - tion brings, let lov - ing hearts en - throne Him.
Refrain
F C/E Am Dm B♭maj7 A
This, this is Christ the King, Whom shep - herds guard and an - gels sing:
F Em7 Am Gm A
1.2.
Dm
Haste, haste to bring him laud, The Babe, the Son of Ma - ry!

3.
C/D
B♭maj7/D
C/D
Dm
1. Why
2. So
Ma - ry!
F
F C/E Dm C7/E
Am7
Dm
B♭maj7
A
Raise, raise the song on high! The Vir - gin sings her lul - la - by.
F
Em
Am
Gm
A
Dm
Joy! joy! for Christ is born, The Babe, the son of Ma - ry!
C/D
B♭maj7/D
C/D
Dm

My Soul Will Magnify the Lord

(The Magnificat)

From Luke 1:46-55
Words and Music by
Keith & Kristyn Getty
and Stuart Townend

With Wonder (𝅗𝅥 = 56)
A Amaj9 D/A Amaj9 Em Bm A
1. My soul will mag - ni - fy the Lord; I re - joice in God my Sav - ior, in the
2. My soul will mag - ni - fy the Lord for His grace to those who fear Him through
G Dmaj7 G A A Amaj9 D/A Amaj9
won - der of His fa - vor. For He has done great things for me; He was
ev - ery gen - er - a - tion. The proud He scat - ters to the wind as the
Em Bm A G Dmaj7 G A
mind - ful of His ser - vant. Ev - ery age shall call me bless - ed. The
ru - ler's strength is bro - ken and the rich are left with noth - ing. The
E/G# A D A Bm Dmaj7 Esus E
Hope of A - bra - ham come in the giv - ing of a Son; for
hum - ble lift - ed high, and the hun - gry sa - tis - fied; Our

E/G♯ A Bm F♯m7 Bm7 Dmaj7 G A
1.
He who prom-ised is might - y in re-mem-ber - ing His mer - cy.
Por-tion and our Trea - sure, our Hope and Help for - ev - er.
2. My
2.
G A
mer - cy.
ev - er.
A Amaj9 D/A Amaj9
rit.
Em/B Bm A G D G A

How Suddenly a Baby Cries

Music by Keith & Kristyn Getty
and Fionán de Barra
(Based on 'The Star of the County Down')
Lyrics by Kristyn Getty

With Energy
Dm C/D B♭maj7/D Am7
1. How sud - den - ly a ba - by cries and all for - ev - er change as
2. She pon - ders how the Ma - gi kneel be - fore Em - man - u el. With
3. What won - der still that An - na, filled with praise, should bless the Lord; Her
4. Hear Sim - e - on who had wait - ed long draw near to hold the child, to
5. How sud - den - ly a ba - by cried and all for - ev - er changed. Through
Dm B♭maj7 Am7 Gm7 Am7 Dm
shep - herds leave the an - gel song to find this ho - ly place, where
gold and frank - in - cense and myrrh, Christ's sac - ri - fice they tell. A
ag - ing eyes now look - ing on the Sav - ior of the world. For
speak of Him who would re - veal the ma - ny thoughts we hide: That
his - t'ry, soul by soul have come to find His heal - ing grace. He
F Am7 Dm Am7
in her young and tremb - ling arms a vir - gin holds her Son. And
dream would help them flee a king whose pride would cruel - ly des - troy. As
night and day her prayers had filled the tem - ple of our God. Her
hearts would rise to know His grace, but ma - ny fall a - way; A
filled my troub - led heart with peace, with hope of end - less worth. My

B♭maj7 Gm7 Am7 B♭maj7 Cadd9 Dm G/D
in this Child of breath di - vine our Light has fin - al - ly come.
moth - ers weep, God's mer - cy meets the hun - ger for His joy.
heart could tell His sav - ing hand with - in this gift of love.
sword would pierce His moth - er's soul up - on re - demp - tion day.
voice will join the song of praise that tells Mes - si - ah's birth.
Dm7 G/D Dm G/D Dm7 G/D
last time
Dm
2. She
3. What
4. Hear
5. How

Joy Has Dawned

Words and Music by
Keith Getty & Stuart Townend

Joyous! (♩ = 128)
F Gm7/F F Csus C Dm7 Gm7 F/C C C7
1. Joy has dawned up - on the world, pro - mised from cre - a - tion–
2. Sounds of won - der fill the sky with the songs of an - gels,
3. Shep - herds bow be - fore the Lamb, gaz - ing at the glo - ry;
4. Son of A - dam, Son of Heav'n, gi - ven as a ran - som;
F Gm7/F F Csus C Dm7 Gm7 Csus C F
God's sal - va - tion now un - furled, hope for ev - 'ry na - tion.
as the might - y Prince of Life shel - ters in a sta - ble.
Gifts of men from dis - tant lands pro - phe - sy the sto - ry.
Re - con - cil - ing God and man, Christ, our might - y cham - pion!
F/A B♭ F/A Gm7 Csus C Dm7 Gm7 F/A F/C C C7
Not with fan - fares from a - bove, not with scenes of glo - ry;
Hands that set each star in place, shaped the earth in dark - ness,
Gold– a King is born to - day, In - cense– God is with us,
What a Sa - vior! What a Friend! What a glo - rious mys - t'ry!

F Gm7 F Csus C Dm7 Gm7 Csus C F
But a hum - ble gift of love– Je - sus born of Ma - ry.
cling now to a moth - er's breast, vul - n'ra - ble and help - less.
Myrrh– His death will make a way and by His blood He'll win us.
Once a babe in Beth - le - hem, Now the Lord of his - t'ry.

last time fine
Gm7 F/A B♭ Dm Csus C F

Jesus, Joy of the Highest Heaven
(The Children's Carol)

Words and Music by
Keith & Kristyn Getty
Descant and Harmony by
Paul Campbell

Slow & Simple (♩ = 66)
Verse 2 Descant/Harmony:
King of Heav - en,
bring us life. Knows our sor - - rows,
a way that is true and right. Je - sus, take a - way ev - ery
D G/D D A/C♯ F♯m7 Bm A G D/F♯ Em7 A7sus4
Dsus D D G/D D A/C♯ F♯m7 Bm A
G D/F♯ Em7 A7sus4 Dsus D G G A G/B D/A D/F♯
1. Je - sus, joy of the high - est Heav - en, born as a lit - tle ba - by un - der a won - drous
2. Je - sus, King of the high - est Heav - en, learn - ing to take His first steps that He might bring us
star. Like us, cry - ing, he takes His first breath, held by His mo - ther,
life. Like us, know - ing our smiles and sor - rows, He showed the way to
help - less, close to her beat - ing heart. Je - sus, laid in a low - ly
fol - low, a way that is true and right. Je - sus, take a - way ev - ery

dark - ness; Stead - y my sim - ple foot - steps that I might, in Your
D/F♯ G Em D/F♯ G D/F♯ D A/C♯ F♯m7 Bm A7
man - ger, fac - ing a world of dan - gers; come to turn me, a
dark - ness; Stead - y my sim - ple foot - steps that I might, in Your
unis.
last time
good - ness, live as a child of God.
G D/F♯ Em7 A7sus4 D G/D D A7sus4/D D G/D D A7sus4/D D
stran - ger, in - to a child of God.
good - ness, live as a child of God.

Carol of the Bells

Wilhousky & Leontovych
with *Young Tom Ennis Jig*
Arranged by Keith Getty
& Fionán de Barra

Lively Celtic Groove (𝅗𝅥. = 58)

Optional Melody instrument (play on repeat):
Cm Gm/B♭ A♭maj7 Gm7
Hark! how the bells, sweet sil - ver bells, all seem to say, "Throw cares a- way."
Cm Gm/B♭ A♭maj7 Gm7
Christ - mas is here, bring - ing good cheer, to young and old, meek and the bold.
Cm Gm/B♭ A♭maj7 Gm7
Ding dong ding dong– that is their song; With joy - ful ring, all ca - rol - ing.
Cm Gm/B♭ A♭maj7 Gm7
One seems to hear words of good cheer from ev - ery-where fill - ing the air.

Cm
Gm/B♭
Fm
Cm
Gai - ly they ring while peo - ple sing songs of good cheer, Christ - mas is here.
G
G
Mer - ry, Mer - ry, Mer - ry, Mer - ry Christ - mas. Mer - ry, Mer - ry, Mer - ry, Mer - ry Christ - mas.
G
G
C5
Mer- ry, Mer- ry, Mer- ry, Mer-ry Christ- mas. Mer- ry, Mer- ry, Mer- ry, Mer-ry Christ- mas.

O Savior of Our Fallen Race

Original Lyrics: Christe Redemptor Omnium,
Latin office hymn, circa 6th Century.
Translated by Gilbert E. Doan, Jr. (1930–),
Adapted by Kristyn Getty

Music by Keith Getty

Steadily (♩ = 72)
Bm F♯m7/A G A Bm
1. O Sav - ior of our fall - en race, O Bright-ness of the Fa - ther's face; O
2. Re - mind us Lord of life and grace how once, to save our fall - en race, You
3. For from the Fa - ther's throne You came, His ba - nished child - ren to re - claim; And
4. O Sav - ior of our fall - en race, the world will see Your ra - diant face for
Bm F♯m7/A G A Bm
Son who shared the Fa - ther's might be - fore the world knew day or night. O
put our hu - man ves - ture on and came to us as Mar - y's son. To -
earth and sea and sky re - vere the love of Him who sent You here. And
You who came to us be - fore will come a - gain and all re - store. Let
E Bm D/A G A Bm D E F♯m7/A
Je - sus ver - y Light of Light Our con - stant star in sin's deep night: Now
day, as year by year its light brings to our world a pro - mise bright, one
we are ju - bi - lant to - day, For You have washed our guilt a - way. O
songs of praise Your name a - dorn, O Christ, Re - deem - er, vir - gin - born whom
Bm F♯m7/A G A 1.2.3. Bm 4. Bm
hear the prayers Your peo - ple pray Through - out the world this ho - ly day. 2. Re -
pre - cious truth out-shines the sun: Sal - va-tion comes from You a - lone. 3. For
hear the glad new song we sing on this, the birth of Christ our King! 4. O
with the Fa - ther we a - dore and Ho - ly Spi - rit ev - er - more.

STORIES BEHIND THE SONGS

Jesus Joy of the Highest Heaven (A Children's Carol)

Keith wrote the melody of this carol for Kristyn when she was pregnant with Eliza. Kristyn then penned the lyrics as a simple carol for children to sing about how Christ became human like us so that we could become children of God. We were very excited to bring together a choir of children from Northern Ireland for this recording.

Carol of the Bells (with Tom Ennis Jig)

This is an Eastern European folk carol with popular lyrics authored by Peter Wilhousky. Fionán de Barra came up with the idea of combining this classic song with an Irish jig called "Tom Ennis Jig!" named after the uilleann piper Tom Ennis. The uilleann pipes often are referred to as the national bagpipe of Ireland and are beautifully played on this album by Skip Cleavinger.

O Savior of Our Fallen Race

Dedicated to the memory of our friend, Chip Stam (1953-2011)

We learned of the text from this sixth century Latin carol through our good friend Eric Wyse. The musical riches of church history from which we can draw never cease to amaze us! Kristyn slightly altered the beautiful translation of Gilbert E. Doan, Jr., with the aim of shaping the song into more of a missional prayer that emphasizes Christ's return. J.A.C. Redford provided this stunning orchestration of Keith's melody, and we hope it will be useful for Christmas and Advent services.

Fullness of Grace

This is a congregational carol based on John 1 that we wrote with Stuart Townend in 2004 as we worked on our Incarnation project. It's actually the first song the three of us wrote together.

Joy to the World (with Miss Eliza's Reel)

The finale of our Christmas concert is "Joy to the World." Interestingly, the English hymn writer and theologian Isaac Watts wrote this song not as a Christmas carol but as a hymn based on Psalm 98. Watts became perhaps the greatest hymn writer of all time and now "Joy to the Word" is the most sung carol in America! We combined it with a reel written by Keith and Fionán named "Miss Eliza's Reel" that finishes the Christmas show with each of the band members showcasing their skills.

An Irish Christmas Blessing

As we think about how words such as peace, hope, love and joy are heard so frequently at Christmas, may our prayer be that their meaning would breathe life into our faith, both during the holiday season and beyond.

Fullness of Grace

Words and Music by
Keith & Kristyn Getty
and Stuart Townend

Slowly, with Wonder (♩ = 78)
Dm Am/C B♭ma7 Am7 Gm7 Am7 B♭ma7 Am/C
1. Full - ness of grace in man's hu-man frail - ty; This is the won-der of Je - sus.
2. Full - ness of grace– the love of the Fa - ther, shown in the face of Je - sus.
3. Full - ness of hope in Christ we had longed for; Pro - mise of God in Je - sus.
Dm Am/C B♭ma7 Am7 Gm7 Am7 Dm
Lay - ing a-side His pow - er and glo - ry hum - bly He en - tered our world.
Stoop - ing to bear the weight of hu-man-i - ty; Walk - ing the Cal - va - ry road.
Through His o - bed - ience we are for - giv - en, op - 'ning the flood-gates of Heav'n.
Gm Dm Gm Dm/A A
Chose the path of mean - est worth; Scan - dal of a vir - gin birth.
Christ, the Ho - ly inn - o - cent took our sin and pun - ish-ment.
All our hopes and dreams we bring glad - ly as an off - er - ing.
Dm Am/C B♭ma7 Am7 Gm7 Am7 Dm
Born in a sta - ble cold and re - jec - ted; here lies the hope of the world.
Full - ness of God, des-pised and re - ject - ed; Crushed for the sins of the world.
Full - ness of life and joy un - speak-a - ble: God's gift in love to the world.

Joy to the World

Lyrics by Isaac Watts
Melody by Lowell Mason
(with themes from George Frideric Handel)
Arranged by Keith Getty and Fionan de Barra

C Fmaj7 G C F G Am7
1. Joy to the world! the Lord is come: Let earth re - ceive her King! Let
2. Joy to the world! the Sav - ior reigns! Let men their songs em - ploy; While
3. No more let sins and sor - rows grow, nor thorns in - fest the ground; He
4. He rules the world with truth and grace, and makes the na - tions prove the
C/G Fmaj7 C/E
ev - 'ry heart pre - pare him room, And heav - en and na - ture sing, and
fields and floods, rocks hills and plains Re - peat the sound - ing joy, re -
comes to make His bless - ings flow far as the curse is found, far
glo - ries of His right - eous - ness, and won - ders of His love, and
Dm G7 E7 Am7 Dm C/E F C/G G
heav - en and na - ture sing, and heav'n and heav'n and na - ture
- peat the sound - ing joy, re - peat, re - peat the sound - ing
as the curse is found, far as, far as the curse is
won - ders of His love, and won - ders, won - ders of His
C F/C B♭/C B♭/C F/C B♭/C F/C C C F/C B♭/C B♭/C F/C B♭/C F/C C C
sing.
joy.
found.
love.

An Irish Christmas Blessing

Words and Music by
Keith & Kristyn Getty
Solo Piano Arranged by Keith Getty

Gently Flowing (♩ = 62)
Em7/D Dmaj7 Em7/D Dmaj7 Em9/D
Solo
p
1. Now may the fra - grance of His
Dmaj9 Em9/D Dmaj9 Em9/D Bm G(add2) D/F♯
peace soar through your heart like the dove re-leased; Hide in His wings, oh wea-ry dis-tant soul– He'll
Em7 A7sus4 Em7/D Dmaj7 Em7/D Dmaj7
guide your spir - it home.
mp
2. And may His
Em7/D Dmaj7 Em7/D Dmaj7 Em7/D
love poured from on high flow to the depths of your deep-est sigh. Oh come and drink from the on-ly

Bm G D/F♯ Em7 A7sus4 Em7/D Dmaj7 Em7/D Dmaj7
liv-ing stream and on His shoul - der lean. 3. And may the
Em7/D Dmaj7 Em7/D Dmaj9 Em7/D
hope that will not de-ceive through ev-ery pain bring e-ter-nal ease. There is no night that can steal the
Bm G D/F♯ Em7 A7sus4 D N.C.
prom-is-es His com-ing brings to us.
Solo
mf sonore
N.C. Em7 Asus rit. A7sus4
f
4. So may His

A Tempo
Em9/D
Dmaj7
Em9/D
Dmaj9
joy rush o - ver you; de - light in the path He has called you to. May all your
p
Em9/D
Bm G(add2) D/F♯
Em7 A7sus4
D(add2)
G/D
steps walk in Heav-en's end-less light be - yond this Christ - mas night.
mf
p dim.
Dmaj7
Gmaj7/D
N.C.
D6/9
8va
Ped.

JOY – An Irish Christmas: The Reels and Jigs

The Star of Munster Reel

(Featured in 'God Rest Ye Merry, Gentlemen')

Am Dm/A Am Dm/A Am Dm/A
1. Dm/A Em7/A 2. Dm/A Em7/A Dm7
G Em7 Fmaj7 Em7 Dm7 Bm7 Em7
Am7
3
Fmaj7 Em7 Dm7 Bm7 Em7 Am

Greengrass Reel

(Featured in 'Hark! The Herald Angels Sing')

Am7 D Am7 C G Am7 D
C G/B G Am7 C G
Am7 D C G/B G D/F♯ Em

Narnian Reel

(Featured in 'How Suddenly a Baby Cries')

Dm Am7 Dm Am7 Cadd9 Dm Am7
1. Gm7 B♭maj7 Cadd9
2. Gm7 Cadd9 Am7 Gm7 Am7
Dm Am7 Gm Am7
1. Gm7 B♭maj7 Am7
2. Gm Am7 Dm

Young Tom Ennis Jig

(Featured in 'Carol of the Bells')

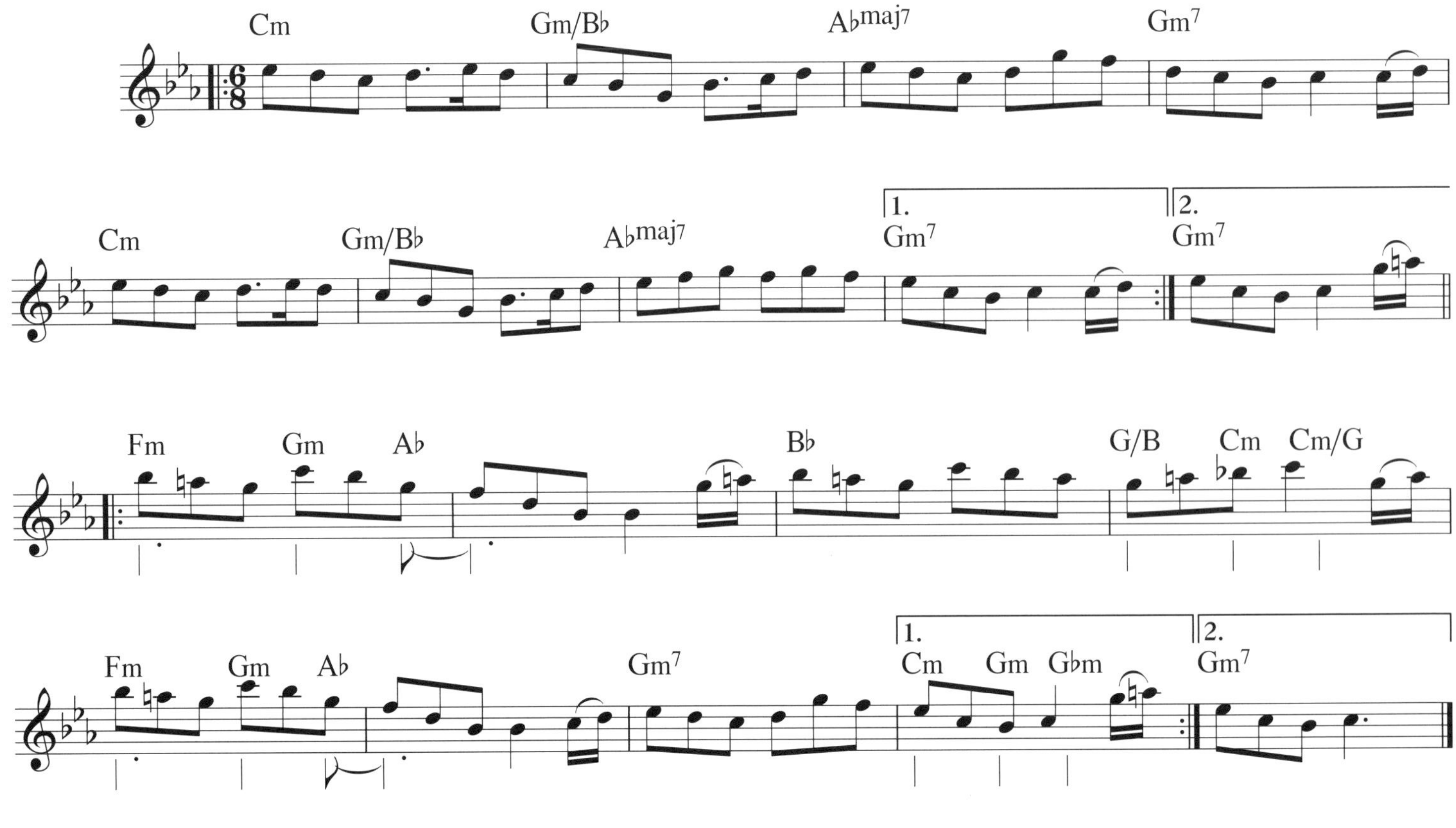
Cm Gm/B♭ A♭maj7 Gm7
Cm Gm/B♭ A♭maj7
1. Gm7
2. Gm7
Fm Gm A♭ B♭ G/B Cm Cm/G
Fm Gm A♭ Gm7
1. Cm Gm G♭m
2. Gm7

Miss Eliza's Reel

(Featured in 'Joy to the World')

A D/A A
A D/A A Em/A
3
A D/A A
Em7 D/A Em7 D/E Em7
A D/A A
3
A D/A A Em/A
G/A D/A A
A Em7 G(add2) A

GETTYMUSIC.COM

BOOKINGS / SONGBOOKS / TRACKS

All songs, stories and further information available from:
gettymusic.com

For touring information contact: **joni@gettymusic.com**
Choral versions available from **gettymusic.com** or **clearcall.com**